MAD LIBS

CHRISTMAS CAROL MAD LIBS

VERY MERRY
SONGS & STORIES

By Roger Price and Leonard Stern

PSS!
PRICE STERN SLOAN

PRICE STERN SLOAN
Published by the Penguin Group
Penguin Group (USA) Inc., 375 Hudson Street, New York, New York 10014, U.S.A.
Penguin Group (Canada), 90 Eglinton Avenue East, Suite 700,
Toronto, Ontario, Canada M4P 2Y3
(a division of Pearson Penguin Canada Inc.)
Penguin Books Ltd, 80 Strand, London WC2R 0RL, England
Penguin Ireland, 25 St Stephen's Green, Dublin 2, Ireland
(a division of Penguin Books Ltd)
Penguin Group (Australia), 250 Camberwell Road, Camberwell,
Victoria 3124, Australia (a division of Pearson Australia Group Pty Ltd)
Penguin Books India Pvt Ltd, 11 Community Centre,
Panchsheel Park, New Delhi - 110 017, India
Penguin Group (NZ), 67 Apollo Drive, Mairangi Bay,
Auckland 1311, New Zealand (a division of Pearson New Zealand Ltd)
Penguin Books (South Africa) (Pty) Ltd, 24 Sturdee Avenue,
Rosebank, Johannesburg 2196, South Africa

Penguin Books Ltd, Registered Offices:
80 Strand, London WC2R 0RL, England

Published by Price Stern Sloan, a division of Penguin Young Readers Group,
345 Hudson Street, New York, New York 10014.

ISBN 978-0-8431-2676-1

3 5 7 9 10 8 6 4 2

MAD LIBS®

INSTRUCTIONS

MAD LIBS® is a game for people who don't like games!
It can be played by one, two, three, four, or forty.

• RIDICULOUSLY SIMPLE DIRECTIONS

In this tablet you will find stories containing blank spaces where words are left out. One player, the READER, selects one of these stories. The READER does not tell anyone what the story is about. Instead, he/she asks the other players, the WRITERS, to give him/her words. These words are used to fill in the blank spaces in the story.

• TO PLAY

The READER asks each WRITER in turn to call out words—adjectives or nouns or whatever the spaces call for—and uses them to fill in the blank spaces in the story. The result is a MAD LIBS® game.

When the READER then reads the completed MAD LIBS® game to the other players, they will discover that they have written a story that is fantastic, screamingly funny, shocking, silly, crazy, or just plain dumb—depending upon which words each WRITER called out.

• EXAMPLE *(Before and After)*

"_____ !" he said _____
      EXCLAMATION   ADVERB

as he jumped into his convertible _____ and
                                             NOUN

drove off with his _____ wife.
                           ADJECTIVE

"_____*Ouch*_____ !" he said _____*stupidly*_____
      EXCLAMATION   ADVERB

as he jumped into his convertible _____*cat*_____ and
                                       NOUN

drove off with his _____*brave*_____ wife.
                           ADJECTIVE

MAD LIBS®

QUICK REVIEW

In case you have forgotten what adjectives, adverbs, nouns, and verbs are, here is a quick review:

An ADJECTIVE describes something or somebody. *Lumpy, soft, ugly, messy,* and *short* are adjectives.

An ADVERB tells how something is done. It modifies a verb and usually ends in "ly." *Modestly, stupidly, greedily,* and *carefully* are adverbs.

A NOUN is the name of a person, place, or thing. *Sidewalk, umbrella, bridle, bathtub,* and *nose* are nouns.

A VERB is an action word. *Run, pitch, jump,* and *swim* are verbs. Put the verbs in past tense if the directions say PAST TENSE. *Ran, pitched, jumped,* and *swam* are verbs in the past tense.

When we ask for A PLACE, we mean any sort of place: a country or city *(Spain, Cleveland)* or a room *(bathroom, kitchen).*

An EXCLAMATION or SILLY WORD is any sort of funny sound, gasp, grunt, or outcry, like *Wow!, Ouch!, Whomp!, Ick!,* and *Gadzooks!*

When we ask for specific words, like a NUMBER, a COLOR, an ANIMAL, or a PART OF THE BODY, we mean a word that is one of those things, like *seven, blue, horse,* or *head.*

When we ask for a PLURAL, it means more than one. For example, *cat* pluralized is *cats.*

MAD LIBS® is fun to play with friends, but you can also play it by yourself! To begin with, DO NOT look at the story on the page below. Fill in the blanks on this page with the words called for. Then, using the words you have selected, fill in the blank spaces in the story.

Now you've created your own hilarious MAD LIBS® game!

JINGLE BELLS

PLURAL NOUN _____

ANIMAL _____

NOUN _____

PLURAL NOUN _____

VERB ENDING IN "ING" _____

PLURAL NOUN _____

PLURAL NOUN _____

VERB _____

PLURAL NOUN _____

SAME PLURAL NOUN _____

VERB _____

SAME ANIMAL _____

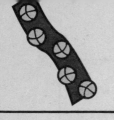

JINGLE BELLS

Dashing through the _____,
PLURAL NOUN

In a one-_____ open _____,
ANIMAL   NOUN

O'er the _____ we go,
PLURAL NOUN

_____ all the way.
VERB ENDING IN "ING"

_____ on bobtails ring,
PLURAL NOUN

Making _____ bright.
PLURAL NOUN

What fun it is to _____ and sing
VERB

A sleighing song tonight!

Jingle _____, jingle _____,
PLURAL NOUN   SAME PLURAL NOUN

Jingle all the way!

Oh, what fun it is to _____
VERB

In a one-_____ open sleigh.
SAME ANIMAL

From CHRISTMAS CAROL MAD LIBS® • Copyright © 2003, 2007 by Price Stern Sloan,
a division of Penguin Young Readers Group, 345 Hudson Street, New York, NY 10014.

MAD LIBS® is fun to play with friends, but you can also play it by yourself! To begin with, DO NOT look at the story on the page below. Fill in the blanks on this page with the words called for. Then, using the words you have selected, fill in the blank spaces in the story.

Now you've created your own hilarious MAD LIBS® game!

GOING CAROLING

ADJECTIVE _____

ADJECTIVE _____

NUMBER _____

ADJECTIVE _____

PLURAL NOUN _____

PLURAL NOUN _____

ADJECTIVE _____

PLURAL NOUN _____

NOUN _____

PLURAL NOUN _____

VERB _____

NUMBER _____

NOUN _____

NUMBER _____

ADVERB _____

NOUN _____

PLURAL NOUN _____

VERB _____

MAD LIBS

GOING CAROLING

'Tis the _____ season for caroling! Here's how to make
        ADJECTIVE

everyone's Christmas a little more merry and _____:
                                ADJECTIVE

- Gather _____ of your _____ friends
        NUMBER   ADJECTIVE

  and family _____ together. Pick out a few classic
         PLURAL NOUN

  _____ to sing, like "Have Yourself a/an
    PLURAL NOUN

  _____ Little Christmas," "Silver _____,"
  ADJECTIVE   PLURAL NOUN

  and "Frosty the _____-man."
           NOUN

- Put Santa _____ on everyone's heads and
          PLURAL NOUN

  _____ to your neighbor's house.
  VERB

- Knock _____ times on the front _____.
       NUMBER   NOUN

  Nothing? Knock _____ more times _____.
         NUMBER   ADVERB

- When your neighbor answers the _____, ask if he
                              NOUN

  or she would like to hear you sing a song. If your neighbor

  says yes, sing your _____ out. If your neighbor says
             PLURAL NOUN

  no, _____ anyway!
    VERB

MAD LIBS® is fun to play with friends, but you can also play it by yourself! To begin with, DO NOT look at the story on the page below. Fill in the blanks on this page with the words called for. Then, using the words you have selected, fill in the blank spaces in the story.

Now you've created your own hilarious MAD LIBS® game!

DECK THE HALLS

PLURAL NOUN _____

PLURAL NOUN _____

NOUN _____

ADJECTIVE _____

ADJECTIVE _____

ADJECTIVE _____

VERB ENDING IN "ING" _____

NOUN _____

ADJECTIVE _____

ADJECTIVE _____

Deck the _____ with boughs of _____,
<small>PLURAL NOUN</small>   <small>PLURAL NOUN</small>

Fa-la-la-la-la-la-la-la-la!

'Tis the _____ to be _____,
<small>NOUN</small>   <small>ADJECTIVE</small>

Fa-la-la-la-la-la-la-la-la!

Don we now our _____ apparel,
<small>ADJECTIVE</small>

Fa-la-la-la-la-la-la-la-la!

Troll the ancient _____ carol,
<small>ADJECTIVE</small>

Fa-la-la-la-la-la-la-la-la!

See the _____ Yule before us,
<small>VERB ENDING IN "ING"</small>

Fa-la-la-la-la-la-la-la-la!

Strike the _____ and join the chorus,
<small>NOUN</small>

Fa-la-la-la-la-la-la-la-la!

Follow me in _____ measure,
<small>ADJECTIVE</small>

Fa-la-la-la-la-la-la-la-la!

While I tell of _____ treasure,
<small>ADJECTIVE</small>

Fa-la-la-la-la-la-la-la-la!

From CHRISTMAS CAROL MAD LIBS® • Copyright © 2003, 2007 by Price Stern Sloan,
a division of Penguin Young Readers Group, 345 Hudson Street, New York, NY 10014.

MAD LIBS® is fun to play with friends, but you can also play it by yourself! To begin with, DO NOT look at the story on the page below. Fill in the blanks on this page with the words called for. Then, using the words you have selected, fill in the blank spaces in the story.

Now you've created your own hilarious MAD LIBS® game!

THE TWELVE DAYS OF CHRISTMAS, PART 1

NOUN _____

NOUN _____

NOUN _____

ADJECTIVE _____

NOUN _____

ADJECTIVE _____

ADJECTIVE _____

NOUN _____

PLURAL NOUN _____

ADJECTIVE _____

NOUN _____

On the first day of Christmas,

My true _____ gave to me
NOUN

A partridge in a/an _____ tree.
NOUN

On the second _____ of Christmas,
NOUN

My _____ love gave to me
ADJECTIVE

Two turtle doves

And a/an _____ in a/an _____ tree.
NOUN　　　　　　　　　　　　ADJECTIVE

On the third day of Christmas,

My _____ _____ gave to me
ADJECTIVE　　　　　　NOUN

Three French hens,

Two turtle _____,
PLURAL NOUN

And a partridge in a/an _____ _____.
ADJECTIVE　　　　　　NOUN

MAD LIBS® is fun to play with friends, but you can also play it by yourself! To begin with, DO NOT look at the story on the page below. Fill in the blanks on this page with the words called for. Then, using the words you have selected, fill in the blank spaces in the story.

Now you've created your own hilarious MAD LIBS® game!

THE TWELVE DAYS OF CHRISTMAS, PART 2

NOUN _____

NUMBER _____

ADJECTIVE _____

NOUN _____

ADJECTIVE _____

NOUN _____

PLURAL NOUN _____

PLURAL NOUN _____

ADJECTIVE _____

PLURAL NOUN _____

ADJECTIVE _____

PLURAL NOUN _____

NOUN _____

ADJECTIVE _____

NOUN _____

MAD LIBS®
THE TWELVE DAYS OF CHRISTMAS, PART 2

On the fourth day of Christmas,

My true _____ gave to me
            NOUN

Four calling birds,

_____ French hens,
        NUMBER

Two _____ doves,
        ADJECTIVE

And a/an _____ in a pear tree.
            NOUN

On the fifth day of Christmas,

My _____ _____ gave to me
      ADJECTIVE   NOUN

Five golden _____ ,
              PLURAL NOUN

Four calling _____ ,
               PLURAL NOUN

Three _____ _____ ,
        ADJECTIVE   PLURAL NOUN

Two _____ _____ ,
      ADJECTIVE   PLURAL NOUN

And a/an _____ in a/an _____ _____ .
            NOUN   ADJECTIVE   NOUN

From CHRISTMAS CAROL MAD LIBS® • Copyright © 2003, 2007 by Price Stern Sloan,
a division of Penguin Young Readers Group, 345 Hudson Street, New York, NY 10014.

MAD LIBS® is fun to play with friends, but you can also play it by yourself! To begin with, DO NOT look at the story on the page below. Fill in the blanks on this page with the words called for. Then, using the words you have selected, fill in the blank spaces in the story.

Now you've created your own hilarious MAD LIBS® game!

CHRISTMAS SHOPPING

ADJECTIVE _____

ADJECTIVE _____

PLURAL NOUN _____

NOUN _____

CELEBRITY _____

VERB (PAST TENSE) _____

VERB _____

ADJECTIVE _____

NOUN _____

TYPE OF LIQUID _____

ADJECTIVE _____

ADJECTIVE _____

NOUN _____

PLURAL NOUN _____

PLURAL NOUN _____

PLURAL NOUN _____

PLURAL NOUN _____

NOUN _____

VERB ENDING IN "ING" _____

MAD LIBS
CHRISTMAS SHOPPING

When I was a/an _____ kid, I loved going to the
ADJECTIVE

_____ mall at Christmastime. My parents would dress me
ADJECTIVE

and my _____ in our cutest holiday outfits. Then we'd all
PLURAL NOUN

pile into the family _____ and drive to the mall to sit on
NOUN

_____'s lap. As we _____ in the long line to Santa's
CELEBRITY   VERB (PAST TENSE)

_____-shop, we'd look around at all the _____
VERB   ADJECTIVE

lights strung around the _____, drink hot _____,
NOUN   TYPE OF LIQUID

and sing _____ carols. Then the _____ moment
ADJECTIVE   ADJECTIVE

would arrive—we'd finally get to meet Santa and tell him what we

wanted to find under the _____ on Christmas morning. Of
NOUN

course, now that I'm older, I avoid the mall at all _____. It's
PLURAL NOUN

so crowded that all the _____ push into one another. You
PLURAL NOUN

can't even catch of glimpse of Santa and his _____. These
PLURAL NOUN

days, I buy all my _____ online. With just a click of the
PLURAL NOUN

_____, Christmas _____ couldn't be easier!
NOUN   VERB ENDING IN "ING"

From CHRISTMAS CAROL MAD LIBS® • Copyright © 2003, 2007 by Price Stern Sloan,
a division of Penguin Young Readers Group, 345 Hudson Street, New York, NY 10014.

MAD LIBS® is fun to play with friends, but you can also play it by yourself! To begin with, DO NOT look at the story on the page below. Fill in the blanks on this page with the words called for. Then, using the words you have selected, fill in the blank spaces in the story.

Now you've created your own hilarious MAD LIBS® game!

THE CHRISTMAS PAGEANT

ADJECTIVE _____

A PLACE _____

PLURAL NOUN _____

PLURAL NOUN _____

ADJECTIVE _____

NOUN _____

NOUN _____

SILLY WORD _____

PERSON IN ROOM (MALE) _____

NOUN _____

ADJECTIVE _____

ADJECTIVE _____

COLOR _____

NOUN _____

ADJECTIVE _____

PART OF THE BODY (PLURAL) _____

PLURAL NOUN _____

SILLY WORD _____

MAD LIBS®
THE CHRISTMAS PAGEANT

Every December, our school puts on a/an _____ holiday
                                          ADJECTIVE
pageant. We decorate (the) _____ with snow-_____
                           A PLACE   PLURAL NOUN
and red and green _____, and we perform a/an
                        PLURAL NOUN
_____ play and sing Christmas carols. This year, the
  ADJECTIVE
_____ is set in the North Pole. Our music _____,
   NOUN   NOUN
Mrs. _____, cast my best friend, _____,
       SILLY WORD   PERSON IN ROOM (MALE)
as Santa. He will, of course, be wearing a red _____ stuffed
                                                   NOUN
with a/an _____ pillow so he'll look really _____.
            ADJECTIVE   ADJECTIVE
I was cast as Rudolph the _____-nosed _____.
                               COLOR   NOUN
I'll be wearing _____ antlers on my _____.
                  ADJECTIVE   PART OF THE BODY (PLURAL)
The rest of the class will be elves making _____ in Santa's
                                              PLURAL NOUN
workshop. I can't wait! Ho, _____, ho!
                               SILLY WORD

From CHRISTMAS CAROL MAD LIBS® • Copyright © 2003, 2007 by Price Stern Sloan,
a division of Penguin Young Readers Group, 345 Hudson Street, New York, NY 10014.

MAD LIBS® is fun to play with friends, but you can also play it by yourself! To begin with, DO NOT look at the story on the page below. Fill in the blanks on this page with the words called for. Then, using the words you have selected, fill in the blank spaces in the story.

Now you've created your own hilarious MAD LIBS® game!

O CHRISTMAS TREE

NOUN _____

SAME NOUN _____

ADJECTIVE _____

SAME NOUN _____

SAME NOUN _____

ADJECTIVE _____

ADJECTIVE _____

PLURAL NOUN _____

ADJECTIVE _____

PLURAL NOUN _____

SAME NOUN _____

SAME NOUN _____

ADJECTIVE _____

MAD LIBS

O CHRISTMAS TREE

O Christmas _____, O Christmas _____,
              NOUN   SAME NOUN

How _____ are your branches!
        ADJECTIVE

O Christmas _____, O Christmas _____,
             SAME NOUN   SAME NOUN

How _____ are your branches!
        ADJECTIVE

They're _____ when summer _____ are bright,
          ADJECTIVE   PLURAL NOUN

They're _____ when winter _____ are white.
          ADJECTIVE   PLURAL NOUN

O Christmas _____, O Christmas _____,
             SAME NOUN   SAME NOUN

How _____ are your branches!
        ADJECTIVE

MAD LIBS® is fun to play with friends, but you can also play it by yourself! To begin with, DO NOT look at the story on the page below. Fill in the blanks on this page with the words called for. Then, using the words you have selected, fill in the blank spaces in the story.

Now you've created your own hilarious MAD LIBS® game!

UP ON THE HOUSETOP

NOUN _____

ANIMAL (PLURAL) _____

ADJECTIVE _____

NOUN _____

ADJECTIVE _____

PERSON IN ROOM _____

PLURAL NOUN _____

EXCLAMATION _____

NOUN _____

VERB _____

PERSON IN ROOM _____

NOUN _____

SILLY WORD _____

SAME SILLY WORD _____

SAME SILLY WORD _____

ADJECTIVE _____

MAD LIBS
UP ON THE HOUSETOP

Up on the _____-top, _____ pause,
             NOUN   ANIMAL (PLURAL)

Out jumps _____ old Santa Claus.
           ADJECTIVE

Down through the _____ with lots of toys,
             NOUN

All for the _____ ones, Christmas joys.
         ADJECTIVE

Ho, ho, ho! Who wouldn't go? Ho, ho, ho! _____ wouldn't go!
                                       PERSON IN ROOM

First comes the _____ of little Nell.
            PLURAL NOUN

_____! Dear Santa, fill it well!
  EXCLAMATION

Give her a/an _____ that laughs and cries,
             NOUN

One that will _____ and shut its eyes.
          VERB

Ho, ho, ho! Who wouldn't go? Ho, ho, ho! _____ wouldn't go!
                                       PERSON IN ROOM

Up on the _____-top, _____, _____,
             NOUN   SILLY WORD   SAME SILLY WORD

_____!
SAME SILLY WORD

Down through the chimney with _____ Saint Nick.
                                 ADJECTIVE

MAD LIBS® is fun to play with friends, but you can also play it by yourself! To begin with, DO NOT look at the story on the page below. Fill in the blanks on this page with the words called for. Then, using the words you have selected, fill in the blank spaces in the story.

Now you've created your own hilarious MAD LIBS® game!

A CHRISTMAS SOLO

NOUN _____

ADVERB _____

ADJECTIVE _____

VERB ENDING IN "ING" _____

NUMBER _____

NOUN _____

VERB (PAST TENSE) _____

COLOR _____

PART OF THE BODY _____

PERSON IN ROOM _____

ADJECTIVE _____

PLURAL NOUN _____

ADJECTIVE _____

PLURAL NOUN _____

ADJECTIVE _____

VERB (PAST TENSE) _____

SAME VERB (PAST TENSE) _____

NOUN _____

ADJECTIVE _____

MAD LIBS
A CHRISTMAS SOLO

A few years ago, my music _____ asked me to sing a
NOUN

Christmas solo at our holiday concert. At first I was _____
ADVERB

flattered, but the more I thought about it, the more _____
ADJECTIVE

I became. Every time I thought about _____ in front
VERB ENDING IN "ING"

of _____ people, my whole _____ started
NUMBER   NOUN

to shake. What if I _____ or forgot the lyrics? What if I
VERB (PAST TENSE)

suddenly developed a/an _____ rash on my _____?
COLOR   PART OF THE BODY

My friend _____ suggested picturing the audience as a
PERSON IN ROOM

bunch of _____ _____ to make it easier. That
ADJECTIVE   PLURAL NOUN

seemed like a/an _____ plan—until I worried I'd start
ADJECTIVE

laughing and all the _____ would think I was _____.
PLURAL NOUN   ADJECTIVE

Finally, the night of the concert arrived. I walked onstage, gathered

all my courage, and _____ like I'd never_____
VERB (PAST TENSE)   SAME VERB (PAST TENSE)

before. The song went off without a/an _____, and I
NOUN

received a standing ovation. It was the most _____ moment
ADJECTIVE

of my entire life!

MAD LIBS® is fun to play with friends, but you can also play it by yourself! To begin with, DO NOT look at the story on the page below. Fill in the blanks on this page with the words called for. Then, using the words you have selected, fill in the blank spaces in the story.

Now you've created your own hilarious MAD LIBS® game!

AUNTIE'S CRAZY CHRISTMAS CLOTHING

PLURAL NOUN _____

PLURAL NOUN _____

ADJECTIVE _____

PERSON IN ROOM (FEMALE) _____

ADJECTIVE _____

PLURAL NOUN _____

PLURAL NOUN _____

PART OF THE BODY _____

PLURAL NOUN _____

COLOR _____

A PLACE _____

NOUN _____

PART OF THE BODY _____

VERB (PAST TENSE) _____

PART OF THE BODY _____

MAD LIBS®
AUNTIE'S CRAZY
CHRISTMAS CLOTHING

Every Christmas, my family gets together to exchange _____
PLURAL NOUN

and eat a big Christmas dinner of ham, mashed _____,
PLURAL NOUN

and all the _____ trimmings. For me, though, the high-
ADJECTIVE

light of every Christmas is seeing my aunt _____
PERSON IN ROOM (FEMALE)

make her _____ entrance. She always wears the craziest
ADJECTIVE

_____ on Christmas. You wouldn't believe it! For
PLURAL NOUN

example, last year she wore earrings that looked like giant Christmas

_____, a sweatshirt with Santa's _____ on the
PLURAL NOUN   PART OF THE BODY

front, and socks with red-and-white candy _____ on them.
PLURAL NOUN

She also wore a snowflake pin with a flashing _____ light
COLOR

that played "Santa Claus Is Coming to (the) _____," and she
A PLACE

carried a/an _____ made out of tinsel. To top it all off, she
NOUN

tied bells to her _____ so she would jingle when she
PART OF THE BODY

_____! Gosh, that was almost as funny as the year she
VERB (PAST TENSE)

wrapped her entire _____ in Christmas lights! I can't wait
PART OF THE BODY

to see what she'll wear this year.

From CHRISTMAS CAROL MAD LIBS® • Copyright © 2003, 2007 by Price Stern Sloan,
a division of Penguin Young Readers Group, 345 Hudson Street, New York, NY 10014.

MAD LIBS® is fun to play with friends, but you can also play it by yourself! To begin with, DO NOT look at the story on the page below. Fill in the blanks on this page with the words called for. Then, using the words you have selected, fill in the blank spaces in the story.

Now you've created your own hilarious MAD LIBS® game!

'TWAS THE NIGHT BEFORE CHRISTMAS, PART 1

NOUN _____

ANIMAL _____

PLURAL NOUN _____

CELEBRITY (MALE) _____

ADJECTIVE _____

NUMBER _____

ADJECTIVE _____

ADJECTIVE _____

SAME CELEBRITY _____

PLURAL NOUN _____

VERB (PAST TENSE) _____

VERB (PAST TENSE) _____

PERSON IN ROOM _____

SILLY WORD _____

SILLY WORD _____

SILLY WORD _____

NOUN _____

VERB _____

VERB _____

VERB _____

'Twas the night before Christmas, when all through the _____,

NOUN

Not a creature was stirring, not even a/an _____.

ANIMAL

The _____ were hung by the chimney with care,

PLURAL NOUN

In hopes that _____ soon would be there.

CELEBRITY (MALE)

When, what to my wondering eyes should appear,

But a/an _____ sleigh and _____ _____

ADJECTIVE   NUMBER   ADJECTIVE
reindeer.

With a little old driver, so _____ and quick,

ADJECTIVE

I knew in a moment it must be _____.

SAME CELEBRITY

More rapid than _____, his reindeer they came,

PLURAL NOUN

As he _____ and _____ and called them by name:

VERB (PAST TENSE)   VERB (PAST TENSE)

"Now, _____! Now, Dancer! Now, _____ and Vixen!

PERSON IN ROOM   SILLY WORD

On, _____! On, Cupid! On, _____ and Blitzen!

SILLY WORD   SILLY WORD

To the top of the _____! To the top of the wall!

NOUN

Now _____ away! _____ away! _____

VERB   VERB   VERB

away, all!"

From CHRISTMAS CAROL MAD LIBS® • Copyright © 2003, 2007 by Price Stern Sloan,
a division of Penguin Young Readers Group, 345 Hudson Street, New York, NY 10014.

MAD LIBS® is fun to play with friends, but you can also play it by yourself! To begin with, DO NOT look at the story on the page below. Fill in the blanks on this page with the words called for. Then, using the words you have selected, fill in the blank spaces in the story.

Now you've created your own hilarious MAD LIBS® game!

'TWAS THE NIGHT BEFORE CHRISTMAS, PART 2

NOUN _____

VERB ENDING IN "ING" _____

VERB ENDING IN "ING" _____

ADJECTIVE _____

CELEBRITY (FROM PART 1) _____

PLURAL NOUN _____

PLURAL NOUN _____

VERB (PAST TENSE) _____

PLURAL NOUN _____

VERB (PAST TENSE) _____

PART OF THE BODY _____

NOUN _____

VERB (PAST TENSE) _____

ADJECTIVE _____

ADJECTIVE _____

And then in a twinkling, I heard on the _____,
NOUN

The _____ and _____ of each _____
VERB ENDING IN "ING"   VERB ENDING IN "ING"   ADJECTIVE

hoof.

And down the chimney _____ came, amid _____
CELEBRITY (FROM PART 1)   PLURAL NOUN

and soot.

He was covered in _____ from his head to his foot.
PLURAL NOUN

He _____ not a word, but went straight to his work,
VERB (PAST TENSE)

And filled all the _____, then _____ with a
PLURAL NOUN   VERB (PAST TENSE)

jerk.

And laying his _____ aside of his nose,
PART OF THE BODY

And giving a nod, up the _____ he rose!
NOUN

But I heard him exclaim as he _____ out of sight,
VERB (PAST TENSE)

"_____ Christmas to all, and to all a/an _____
ADJECTIVE   ADJECTIVE

night!"

MAD LIBS® is fun to play with friends, but you can also play it by yourself! To begin with, DO NOT look at the story on the page below. Fill in the blanks on this page with the words called for. Then, using the words you have selected, fill in the blank spaces in the story.

Now you've created your own hilarious MAD LIBS® game!

TOYLAND

NOUN _____

NOUN _____

NOUN _____

VERB _____

ADJECTIVE _____

NOUN _____

ADJECTIVE _____

ADJECTIVE _____

PLURAL NOUN _____

Toyland, _____-land,

NOUN

Little _____ and _____ land,

NOUN   NOUN

While you _____ within it,

VERB

You are ever _____ there.

ADJECTIVE

_____'s joy land,

NOUN

_____, _____ Toyland!

ADJECTIVE   ADJECTIVE

Once you pass its _____,

PLURAL NOUN

You can never return again.

From CHRISTMAS CAROL MAD LIBS® • Copyright © 2003, 2007 by Price Stern Sloan,
a division of Penguin Young Readers Group, 345 Hudson Street, New York, NY 10014.

MAD LIBS® is fun to play with friends, but you can also play it by yourself! To begin with, DO NOT look at the story on the page below. Fill in the blanks on this page with the words called for. Then, using the words you have selected, fill in the blank spaces in the story.

Now you've created your own hilarious MAD LIBS® game!

JOLLY OLD SAINT NICHOLAS

ADJECTIVE _____

PART OF THE BODY _____

NOUN _____

ADJECTIVE _____

NUMBER _____

NOUN _____

ADVERB _____

PLURAL NOUN _____

VERB ENDING IN "ING" _____

ADJECTIVE _____

PLURAL NOUN _____

NOUN _____

ADJECTIVE _____

VERB (PAST TENSE) _____

ADJECTIVE _____

Jolly _____ Saint Nicholas, lean your _____ this
        ADJECTIVE   PART OF THE BODY

way!

Don't you tell a single _____ what I'm going to say.
                        NOUN

Christmas Eve is coming soon; now you dear _____ man,
                                           ADJECTIVE

Whisper what you'll bring to me; tell me if you can.

When the clock is striking _____, when I'm fast asleep,
                           NUMBER

Down the chimney with your _____, _____
                           NOUN   ADVERB

you will creep.

All the _____ you will find, _____ in a row;
        PLURAL NOUN   VERB ENDING IN "ING"

Mine will be the _____ one—you'll be sure to know.
                 ADJECTIVE

Johnny wants a pair of _____, Susie wants a/an
                       PLURAL NOUN

_____,
NOUN

Nellie wants a/an _____ book—one she hasn't _____.
                 ADJECTIVE   VERB (PAST TENSE)

Now I think I'll leave to you what to give the rest.

Choose for me, _____ Santa Claus. You will know the
               ADJECTIVE

best.

MAD LIBS® is fun to play with friends, but you can also play it by yourself! To begin with, DO NOT look at the story on the page below. Fill in the blanks on this page with the words called for. Then, using the words you have selected, fill in the blank spaces in the story.

Now you've created your own hilarious MAD LIBS® game!

OVER THE RIVER AND THROUGH THE WOOD

CELEBRITY _____

NOUN _____

NOUN _____

ADJECTIVE _____

ADJECTIVE _____

NOUN _____

NOUN _____

VERB _____

PART OF THE BODY (PLURAL) _____

PART OF THE BODY _____

NOUN _____

NOUN _____

NOUN _____

PLURAL NOUN _____

SILLY WORD _____

Over the river and through the wood,

To _____'s house we go.
CELEBRITY

The _____ knows the way to carry the _____
NOUN   NOUN

Through the _____ and _____ snow.
ADJECTIVE   ADJECTIVE

Over the _____ and through the _____,
NOUN   NOUN

Oh, how the wind does _____.
VERB

It stings the _____ and bites the _____
PART OF THE BODY (PLURAL)   PART OF THE BODY

As over the _____ we go.
NOUN

Over the river and through the _____,
NOUN

To have a full _____ of play.
NOUN

Oh, hear the _____ ringing _____-a-ling-ling,
PLURAL NOUN   SILLY WORD

For it is Christmas Day!

MAD LIBS® is fun to play with friends, but you can also play it by yourself! To begin with, DO NOT look at the story on the page below. Fill in the blanks on this page with the words called for. Then, using the words you have selected, fill in the blank spaces in the story.

Now you've created your own hilarious MAD LIBS® game!

THE NAUGHTY LIST

ADJECTIVE _____

NOUN _____

ADJECTIVE _____

ADVERB _____

PLURAL NOUN _____

NOUN _____

PLURAL NOUN _____

ADJECTIVE _____

PLURAL NOUN _____

NOUN _____

PART OF THE BODY (PLURAL) _____

NOUN _____

NOUN _____

ADJECTIVE _____

SAME ADJECTIVE _____

MAD LIBS®
THE NAUGHTY LIST

Make sure you are always a/an _____ little girl or boy, or
ADJECTIVE

you might get a lump of coal in your _____ at Christmas!
NOUN

Here is a list of _____ things to do and *not* to do to stay off
ADJECTIVE

Santa's naughty list:

ALWAYS play _____ with your brothers and/or sisters and
ADVERB

share your _____ with them.
PLURAL NOUN

NEVER make a mess and then blame it on your pet _____.
NOUN

ALWAYS eat your green _____—even if they taste like
PLURAL NOUN

_____ _____.
ADJECTIVE   PLURAL NOUN

ALWAYS make your _____ and brush your
NOUN

_____ every morning.
PART OF THE BODY (PLURAL)

NEVER tell your teacher that your _____ ate your
NOUN

homework—unless, of course, you can bring in a well-chewed

_____ as proof.
NOUN

And always remember: Santa knows when you've been bad or

_____, so be _____, for goodness' sake!
ADJECTIVE   SAME ADJECTIVE

From CHRISTMAS CAROL MAD LIBS® • Copyright © 2003, 2007 by Price Stern Sloan,
a division of Penguin Young Readers Group, 345 Hudson Street, New York, NY 10014.

MAD LIBS® is fun to play with friends, but you can also play it by yourself! To begin with, DO NOT look at the story on the page below. Fill in the blanks on this page with the words called for. Then, using the words you have selected, fill in the blank spaces in the story.

Now you've created your own hilarious MAD LIBS® game!

FAVORITE CHRISTMAS CAROLS

ADVERB _____

VERB ENDING IN "ING" _____

ADJECTIVE _____

ADJECTIVE _____

NOUN _____

CELEBRITY _____

COLOR _____

VERB _____

NOUN _____

NOUN _____

NOUN _____

COLOR _____

NOUN _____

MAD LIBS®
FAVORITE CHRISTMAS CAROLS

Here's a list of the top ten most _____ played Christmas
ADVERB

carols. Which one is your favorite?

1) "The Christmas Song" ("Chestnuts _____ on a/an
VERB ENDING IN "ING"

_____ Fire")
ADJECTIVE

2) "Have Yourself a Merry _____ Christmas"
ADJECTIVE

3) "_____ Wonderland"
NOUN

4) "_____ Is Coming to Town"
CELEBRITY

5) "_____ Christmas"
COLOR

6) "Let It _____"
VERB

7) "Jingle _____ Rock"
NOUN

8) "Little Drummer _____"
NOUN

9) "_____ Ride"
NOUN

10) "Rudolph the _____-Nosed _____"
COLOR   NOUN

MAD LIBS® is fun to play with friends, but you can also play it by yourself! To begin with, DO NOT look at the story on the page below. Fill in the blanks on this page with the words called for. Then, using the words you have selected, fill in the blank spaces in the story.

Now you've created your own hilarious MAD LIBS® game!

WE WISH YOU A MERRY CHRISTMAS

ADJECTIVE _____

SAME ADJECTIVE _____

SAME ADJECTIVE _____

ADJECTIVE _____

ADJECTIVE _____

PLURAL NOUN _____

ADJECTIVE _____

ADJECTIVE _____

ADJECTIVE _____

SAME ADJECTIVE _____

SAME ADJECTIVE _____

NOUN _____

VERB _____

SAME VERB _____

SAME VERB _____

VERB _____

We wish you a/an _____ Christmas,
　　　　　　　　　　　ADJECTIVE

We wish you a/an _____ Christmas,
　　　　　　　　　　　SAME ADJECTIVE

We wish you a/an _____ Christmas
　　　　　　　　　　　SAME ADJECTIVE

And a/an _____ New Year.
　　　　　ADJECTIVE

_____ tidings we bring
ADJECTIVE

To you and your _____,
　　　　　　　　PLURAL NOUN

_____ tidings for Christmas
ADJECTIVE

And a/an _____ New Year.
　　　　　ADJECTIVE

Oh, bring us a/an _____ pudding,
　　　　　　　　　ADJECTIVE

Oh, bring us a/an _____ pudding,
　　　　　　　　　SAME ADJECTIVE

Oh, bring us a/an _____ pudding
　　　　　　　　　SAME ADJECTIVE

And a cup of good _____.
　　　　　　　　　NOUN

We won't _____ until we get some,
　　　　　VERB

We won't _____ until we get some,
　　　　　SAME VERB

We won't _____ until we get some,
　　　　　SAME VERB

So _____ some out here.
　　VERB

MAD LIBS® is fun to play with friends, but you can also play it by yourself! To begin with, DO NOT look at the story on the page below. Fill in the blanks on this page with the words called for. Then, using the words you have selected, fill in the blank spaces in the story.

Now you've created your own hilarious MAD LIBS® game!

A CHRISTMAS BLIZZARD

ADJECTIVE _____

ADJECTIVE _____

PLURAL NOUN _____

ADJECTIVE _____

VERB ENDING IN "ING" _____

ADJECTIVE _____

NOUN _____

NOUN _____

NOUN _____

NOUN _____

NOUN _____

NOUN _____

ADJECTIVE _____

MAD LIBS

A CHRISTMAS BLIZZARD

Have you been dreaming of a/an _____ Christmas? Me too!
                              ADJECTIVE

But what do you do when there is a/an _____ blizzard and
                                       ADJECTIVE

you and your _____ get snowed in on Christmas? Here's
             PLURAL NOUN

a/an _____ list of classic Christmas movies that'll keep
     ADJECTIVE

everyone _____ for hours.
         VERB ENDING IN "ING"

1) *It's a/an* _____ *Life*
              ADJECTIVE

2) *Miracle on 34th* _____
                     NOUN

3) *A Christmas* _____
                 NOUN

4) *How the* _____ *Stole Christmas*
             NOUN

5) *Frosty the Snow-*_____
                     NOUN

So just grab some pop-_____, throw a few more logs on
                      NOUN

the _____, and keep dreaming of a/an _____
    NOUN   ADJECTIVE

white Christmas!

MAD LIBS® is fun to play with friends, but you can also play it by yourself! To begin with, DO NOT look at the story on the page below. Fill in the blanks on this page with the words called for. Then, using the words you have selected, fill in the blank spaces in the story.

Now you've created your own hilarious MAD LIBS® game!

HERE WE COME A-CAROLING

PLURAL NOUN _____

ADJECTIVE _____

VERB ENDING IN "ING" _____

ADJECTIVE _____

PLURAL NOUN _____

ADJECTIVE _____

ADJECTIVE _____

ADJECTIVE _____

NOUN _____

MAD LIBS®

HERE WE COME A-CAROLING

Here we come a-caroling among the _____ so
_____ PLURAL NOUN

_____.
ADJECTIVE

Here we come a-_____ so _____ to be seen.
VERB ENDING IN "ING"   ADJECTIVE

Love and _____ come to you.
PLURAL NOUN

And to you _____ Christmas, too.
ADJECTIVE

And we wish you and send you a/an _____ New Year.
ADJECTIVE

And we wish you a/an _____ New _____.
ADJECTIVE   NOUN

This book is published by

PSS!
PRICE STERN SLOAN

whose other splendid titles include such literary classics as

The Original #1 Mad Libs®

Son of Mad Libs®

Sooper Dooper Mad Libs®

Monster Mad Libs®

Goofy Mad Libs®

Off-the-Wall Mad Libs®

Vacation Fun Mad Libs®

Camp Daze Mad Libs®

Christmas Fun Mad Libs®

Dinosaur Mad Libs®

Mad Libs® 40th Anniversary Deluxe Edition

Mad Mad Mad Mad Mad Libs®

Mad Libs® On the Road

The Apprentice™ Mad Libs®

The Powerpuff Girls™ Mad Libs®

Scooby-Doo!™ Mad Libs®

Flushed Away™ Mad Libs®

Happy Feet™ Mad Libs®

Madagascar™ Mad Libs®

Over the Hedge™ Mad Libs®

Operation™ Mad Libs®

SpongeBob SquarePants™ Mad Libs®

Fear Factor™ Mad Libs®

Fear Factor™ Mad Libs®: Ultimate Gross Out!

Survivor™ Mad Libs®

Guinness World Records™ Mad Libs®

Betty and Veronica® Mad Libs®

Napoleon Dynamite™ Mad Libs®

Nancy Drew® Mad Libs®

The Mad Libs® Worst-Case Scenario™ Survival Handbook

The Mad Libs® Worst-Case Scenario™ Survival Handbook 2

and many, many more!

Mad Libs® are available wherever books are sold.